Victorian and Edwardian
FIELD SPORTS
from old photographs

1 New Year's Day meet of the South Berkshire at
Streatley House, in 1902. The hunt was founded in 1843.

Victorian and Edwardian

FIELD
SPORTS

from old photographs

Introduction and commentaries by

J.N.P. WATSON

B.T. Batsford Ltd · *London*

This book is dedicated to, by permission, the
British Field Sports Society by whose care and
vigilance most of the country sports enjoyed by our
grandparents and great-grandparents still prosper
today.

© J.N.P. Watson 1978
First published 1978

ISBN 0 7134 1484 7

Filmset in 'Monophoto' Apollo by
Servis Filmsetting Limited, Manchester

Printed in Great Britain by The Anchor Press Ltd,
Tiptree, Essex
for the publishers B.T. Batsford Limited
4 Fitzhardinge Street London W1H 0AH

Contents

Acknowledgement

I am grateful to the Editor of *Country Life* for allowing illustration numbers 129, 146 and 150 to be reproduced from the magazine's photographic library, and the following from *Country Life* issues between 1898 and 1907: 7, 10–19, 21, 22, 28, 43, 47, 50, 55, 57–60, 63, 65, 69, 75, 78–80, 82–85, 88–90, 92, 94, 95, 102, 103, 105–12, 114–17, 120–23, 125–27, 134–37, 139, 141–43, 153, 155, 156, 158–60. My thanks are also due to Mrs Ursula Rayska for illustrations 48 and 151; Mr John Tarlton for 149; Messrs Purdey and Sons Ltd (Gunmakers) for 98, 101, and 119; the Radio Times Hulton Picture Library for 4, 5, 6, 8, 9, 24, 49, 51–53, 64, 68, 70, 71, 81, 104, 118, 130–32, 138, 140, 144, 145, 147, and 148; the Mansell Collection for 56, 66, 67, 74, 86, 113 and 124; Popperfoto for 97, 99 and 100; the Museum of English Rural Life for 87, 128 and 133; the Central Libraries, Birmingham for 3; and Oxfordshire County Council for 1 and 154.

The following books were also used to provide illustrations: *King Edward VII as Sportsman* by A.E.T. Watson for 41 and 96; *Game and Gunroom Notes* by 'Blagdon' for 91 and 93; *The Country Life Library of Sport* for 152 and 157 (all three of which were published prior to 1914); *Harehunters All* for 76 and 77 (published about 1940); and *British Hunts and Huntsmen* (published in 1909) for 20, 23, 25–27, 31, 32–34, 44–46, 61 and 62.

I must also thank my wife, Lavinia, who, as ever, did all the typing for the manuscript.

J.N.P. WATSON

Introduction

THE HUNTER'S INSTINCT

The pursuit of bird, beast and fish was mankind's first activity. With simple traps, flint-headed spears, ropes of tree-bark and crude hooks and bait, prehistoric man outwitted and outran his quarry, or fished it from the lakes and rivers. He drew the creatures of the chase on the walls of his caves; he loved them, even worshipped them. The ancients evolved the bow and arrow into a weapon that could find an animal's heart at several hundred yards; they bred horses that were capable of overhauling all but the fleetest mammals, and they developed the racing chariot; they trained falcons to pull down birds from the sky and pluck fleeing animals from the ground for them; and, from the wild dog and the wolf, they bred hounds that hunted by sight or by scent, in pairs or in packs.

Medieval man invented gunpowder and, by the eighteenth century, had fashioned a hand-weapon that took birds on the wing and animals at the run. Although, with the overwintering of cattle and the overall growth of agriculture, it was no longer essential to hunt for food, the primitive instinct, the thrill of the chase, and the triumph of seizing the quarry remained. Neither the partridges which eighteenth-century man shot, nor the fish for which he cast his line, were necessary for his survival. Nor was it any longer vital to himself and his family that his deerhounds took the stag they chased. The rabbit, whose life ended in the trained peregrine's talons, was

2 An 1869 group of the Tiverton. Left to right: Mr Chichester Nagle, Mr Thomas Carew, Capt. Walter Carew, Squire Besley, Mr William Rayer, Mr W.P. Collier, Mr Thomas Beedle, Mr Thomas Clarke, Mr John Heathcot Amory, the Rev. G.W. Owen and Mr Frank Cockburn. A Devon hunt, the Tiverton emerged from a family pack kept by the Troyte family.

fed to the bird itself. The primeval urge to hunt, to kill and eat was transmuted into the joys of outwitting and outpacing the animal, foiling the fish and bringing it to land, the quick skill of the shot, the exhilaration and exciting uncertainty of a day with dogs and horses, a day closely involved with wild Nature. Compassion for animals had been growing. Recognised as callous and unnatural, bull- and bear-baiting were made illegal in 1835 and cock-fighting in 1840. Men were determined that the least possible cruelty should occur in their sport, whether it was a means of vermin control or not. But hunting, shooting and fishing were the imitation of Nature. Nature is cruel, they said, and Man is Nature's child.

Perhaps the accolade most cherished by Victorian and Edwardian countrymen and women was that of 'good sportsman' or 'good sportswoman'. That was to say – strictly within the written and unwritten rules and codes of conduct – a courageous follower of hounds, an energetic and accomplished game-shot or stalking rifle, fisher, harecourser or falconer. The prosperity coming with the Industrial Revolution opened up the whole spectrum of country sports to an

infinitely wider field of society. And, since being a 'sportsman' brought with it a certain social distinction, the new rich stood to win esteem of another kind. Nor is it difficult, among some of these photographs, to distinguish the sportsmen with ambitions from those who were thoroughly assured of and satisfied with their place in society.

ABOVE
3 Wondering whether there would be a scent and other imponderables.

4 A group of tenant farmers at a meet of the Cotswold at Cowley Manor, Gloucestershire. The bowler hats, dark breeches and black coats signify their station.

8

Foxhunting

In England, up to the end of the seventeenth century, the deer was the 'King of all venery'. His demise began under the Commonwealth, when the old Royal Forests were confiscated and their game laws removed. Increasing inroads were also being made for house- and ship-building in Britain's woodlands. As a result, the deer, fast losing its habitat, also lost its position in the hierarchy of the chase, while that small swift creature of open plain and field, the hare, went into the lead. Most of the English squires kept a kennelful of harriers, slow, patient hounds with strong noses which could stay latched to the scent all day if necessary, until they practically wore their pilot to a standstill.

The fox had long been recognised as a worthy quarry, but, once he had a reasonable start, the old English hounds – the Southern-mouthed (as they were called), descendants of the Gascons of South-west France – were too slow to catch him, so they tracked him to his earth, where he was dug out. It was not until the 1750s – when the Leicestershire squire, Hugo Meynell, with one or two other foxhunting enthusiasts, made a number of experiments in crossing the Southern hound with the Northern beagle, a fleet-footed hound with greyhound blood, but one lacking in voice and nose – that a foxhound

combining stamina and drive with all the other qualities was evolved, a hound able to keep well ahead of galloping horses and, after long and exciting runs, to catch its foxes in the open. Then the Napoleonic wars gave the impetus to a fresh agricultural drive, resulting in the Enclosure Acts. In lowland Britain, these Acts caused the number of hedges, timber fences, walls and ditches to be increased threefold, and the jumping of these obstacles added very considerably to the quality of the sport.

Foxhunting had long been a leading sport in the Lakeland fells, where shepherds, miners, millers, roadbuilders and other ordinary folk followed trencher-fed packs on foot, and in Wales and the West Country, where gaitered farmers, riding unclipped ponies, supported the bobbery packs. But now, with the turn of the eighteenth century, it became England's premier fashionable sport, and, by the time the earliest photographs in these pages were taken, the British Isles were largely divided into hunt countries with well defined boundaries. A uniform, which remains the principal dress today, was worn, combining a silk top hat (velvet cap for Masters and hunt servants), a scarlet coat (black for clerics and the same, eventually, with bowler hats, for farmers) with buttons embossed with the hunt crest, a white neck-

stock, white breeches, mahogany-top boots (a legacy from the old thigh boot, turned down) and a whip with a thong, with which to hold off cattle and sheep, open gates and, possibly, help to control hounds.

Codes of conduct were drawn up to protect both the farmland and the hounds and to maintain standards of behaviour and the honour of the hunt. Foxhunting became a status symbol. The tenant farmers followed the squirearchy; and so, too, did the rich merchants and business men (the Industrial Revolution's potential recruits for the ranks of the upper classes) go hunting, either out of genuine sportsmanship or to pose as country gentlemen. In spite of the suffocating nature of Victorian decorousness, women started joining the hunt in the 1860s, and it was not long before the children followed. By the 1870s at least 10,000 people were riding to hounds, with about the same number following on foot.

The march of industry, technology and agricultural improvement brought mixed blessings. Chemical and fish fertilisers spoiled the scent; wire, which first appeared about 1860, and barbed wire about 1880, restricted movement; while land drainage and steam ploughing rendered cross-country riding much easier. Beginning with Stephenson's Stockton to Darlington line in 1826, the railways, like the canals, seemed to pose a dreadful threat to the sport. But, as barriers, they proved quite surmountable, and their amenity gave foxhunting a considerable boost. For, although they brought the great coaching system, and with it the travellers' inns, into decline, the trains did enable townsmen to get to and from their day's hunting within the day, and livery stables were soon established at all the hunting countries' principal towns. By the late Victorian and Edwardian era, subscriptions were being taken in most countries, and, having long subscribers' lists, Masters could rely on generous guarantees, so that substantial packs could be maintained on a basis of three, four or five hunting days a week. Experienced and hard-working hunt servants were handsomely paid and provided for, and handsomely mounted, too. Also, by arrangement with the landowners, at a price, wire could be taken down in the autumn and put up again in the spring.

Many old-school Edwardians opined that the motor-car would eventually transform foxhunting from a proper hardy sport into a soft one, and we must imagine most of the followers portrayed in these pages hacking many miles to the meet and many miles home again from the day's hunting.

5 The Bicester and Warden Hill at Souldern Gate, Brackley, in 1905. Their country – in Oxfordshire, Buckinghamshire and Northamptonshire – was first formed in the 1770s, by John Warde, who was known as 'the Father of Foxhunting', and was more firmly established by Sir Thomas Mostyn in 1800.

AT THE MEET

6 The same hunt meeting three years later, in November.

ABOVE

7 From pony-trap to sidesaddle in 1898. Before the First World War, it was considered indecent for women to ride astride. The sidesaddle has two pommels on the nearside, over one of which the rider rests her right leg. She places her left leg under the lower pommel.

8 The high Shires: smart dialogue at a Cottesmore meet. The Shire packs – of Leicestershire, Rutlandshire, Northamptonshire and Lincolnshire were the Belvoir, Cottesmore, Fernie, Pytchley and Quorn.

9 Moving off to the first draw: Atherstone followers in 1905.

10 At the first draw: her second horseman checks her girth.

11   Before the days of the 'forward seat': over a hedge-topped bank in Leicestershire, 1899.

IN THE FIELD

12   Clearing a stake-and-bound in the provinces, 1901.

13   Three together over a thorn fence.

14   Jumping big over the water.

15 Sidesaddle across a tumbled
five-bar gate, 1902.

16 Going hard at the blackthorn.

17 1910: an Atherstone follower jumping a stake-and-bound with a ditch in front.

18 The leaders hard on the line of their fox from a 1900 meet.

19 1901: a fox to ground.

AT THE KENNELS AND STABLES

20 The Southdown bitches in 1908. Three years later Norman Loder (alias Denis Milden in Siegfried Sassoon's *Memoirs of a Foxhunting Man*) became Master of this hunt, and – said Sassoon – 'asserted his independence by getting rid of the dog-pack, of which the members had always prided themselves so much'.

21 A morning-after visit to the stables.

22 Lord Lonsdale, 'The Yellow Earl', (left) seeing his horses off a train during his Mastership of the Quorn in 1898. His huntsman Tom Firr, perhaps the most famous hunt servant of his time, was sent on to meets in a yellow chaise.

GREAT MASTERS AND OTHERS

OPPOSITE
24 'The Yellow Earl' as Master of the Cottesmore in 1908. He laid on a fleet of yellow carriages to convey his house-parties to the meets.

23 A foxhunter with the knee-boots of the early Victorian era: Sir William Fitzherbert Bt., who was for 70 years a follower of the Meynell in Derbyshire and Staffordshire.

25 A distinguished hound-breeder and amateur huntsman: C.B.E. Wright. He was Master of the Badsworth (Yorkshire) from 1876 to 1892 and afterwards of the Old Berkshire.

26 Squire Farquharson, a protegé of the great eighteenth-century hunting authority, Peter Beckford, and known as 'The Meynell of the West', hunted the whole of Dorset and parts of Somerset and Wiltshire from 1806 to 1856.

27 Parson Jack Russell, the ardent West Country venerer of stag, fox, otter and hare, was a friend of the Prince of Wales, and breeder of the celebrated terrier, the Jack Russell. Parson Russell died in 1883.

28 A retirement photograph of T.C. Garth. In 1852 he established in Berkshire what was to become famous as 'Mr Garth's country', and retired 50 seasons later. (The Garth merged with the South Berkshire in 1962.)

29 Nicholas Snow, founder, in the 1870s, of the Exmoor Hunt. His hounds were known, from their predominant whiteness, as 'The Stars of the West'.

30 Mr John Watson, Master of the
Meath, 1891–1908. Son and grandson
of Irish Masters, pioneer of polo and
brilliant amateur huntsman, he was
famous throughout Ireland as 'the
Great John Watson'.

31 Swallowtail perfection in
Ireland: the Earl of Kenmare, a
Duhallow follower.

32 An American, who made his name in Ireland: Mr Isaac Bell, arguably the most famous name in modern foxhunting. Master of the Galway Blazers (1903–8) and the Kilkenny (from 1908), "Ikey" Bell was the first hound-breeder to break away from the heavy Belvoir type by introducing Welsh blood, and this eventually led to the lighter, more agile and lower-scenting modern hound.

33 Sir Gilbert Greenall took over the Mastership of the Belvoir when the dynasty of the Dukes of Rutland ended in 1896.

34 Brothers who formed the joint-Mastership of the Linlithgow and Stirlingshire from 1895 to 1906: Robert, Fred and Frank Usher. The L and S is Scotland's oldest County hunt.

35 James Treadwell. He was huntsman to Squire Farquharson from 1837 to 1858.

36 A huntsman of the 1850s on hound exercise.

28

37 Stephen Dobson, huntsman to the Essex Hounds,
1867–79.

James Cooper (1859–70)

38–40   Famous huntsmen of the Belvoir heyday

Ben Capell (1896–1912)

Frank Gillard (1870–96)

FOLLOWERS

41 The Prince and Princess of Wales shortly after their marriage in 1862. The Prince was an ardent and ubiquitous foxhunter before he became overweight. Then pheasant shooting became his favourite sport.

42 A hunting-field beauty of the 1870s and 1880s: Lady Randolph Churchill. Daughter of New Yorker Leonard Jerome and mother of Winston, she was a regular follower of the Meath and other Irish packs when her father-in-law, the Duke of Marlborough, was Lord Lieutenant there.

Miss Nolans (Island)

Mrs Mowbray (Queen's County).

LEFT
Lady Louth, wife of the 14th Baron, a follower of the Louth and other Irish packs

46 Miss Pinckney, of the Wilton.

47 Mrs Seymour Dubourg and friend. Her husband was Master of the South Berkshire from 1894 to 1910.

48 Beauty and ewe-necked beast: Lady Leighton at Loton Park, Shropshire.

THE YOUNG

49 Youthful foxhunters prepared for a day with the Atherstone in 1910. Miss Marjorie and (right) Miss Edith Loder.

50 Somewhere in the Shires, 1898.

51 Miss Morton and her pony, West Norfolk Hunt, 1910.

52 Forester and Milbank children with mothers, nannies and friends at the traditional Quorn opening meet, Kirby Gate, Leicestershire.

53 A West Norfolk foot follower making friends: Diana Howard.

OPPOSITE
54 Typical Fell country huntsmen of the 1890s. The first hounds in the world to be entered to fox only may have been those in the Lake District, where the hunting was nearly all on foot. Hounds were trencher-fed in the summer, that is to say kept and fed by individual farmers and others, and were often kept on this basis in the winter, too, when they would be taken to the meets in their twos and threes.

Deerhunting

Foxhunting had by no means put the other branches of venery into eclipse. Dedicated riders to hounds in the West Country would follow one of the packs of staghounds from August to October, and those living in a staghunting country continued the season with hind-hunting between November and February. The procedure in staghunting then, as now, was that the 'harbourer' reported to the Master where he thought the stag was lurking. The bulk of the hounds were kept back while a few old and tried hounds, the 'tufters', drew the covert and drove the stag into the open.

In the New Forest, four packs hunted the fallow deer. A few packs were kept to hunt the carted deer (which was usually kept in a kennel next to the hounds) notably the Queen's Buckhounds, whose country was the Windsor area, and whose staff wore the Royal livery.

56 A big turn-out for an 1895 meet. The red deer was only hunted in the West Country.

55 The Devon and Somerset Staghounds on the Quantocks, in 1898. The hunt was founded by the Acland family in the eighteenth century.

57 Her Majesty's Buckhounds, huntsman, and whipper-in. From Windsor they hunted the carted deer in Berkshire, Buckinghamshire and Surrey.

58 Lord Coventry (in the top hat), the Master, leading
the Royal-liveried hunt servants to meet the deer-cart.

59 Followers crossing a ford from a meet near Windsor.

60 Uncarting, 1899.

62 Proud Master of the South Coast Staghounds: Mr Kay. His hounds hunted the carted fallow deer.

61 Lord Ribblesdale. Blooded to wild stag in the Forest of Fontainebleau under the Second Empire as a boy, Ribblesdale became Master of the Royal Buckhounds in the 1890s. His portrait by Sargent hangs in the Tate.

Otterhunting

The hunting of otters with hounds was an ancient sport going back to early Norman times. Only a century ago, otters were so plentiful as to be a menace to fishermen, and were regarded as vermin. In 1890 there were nine packs, three of these being in Scotland, Cumberland and Westmorland, three in Wales, three in south-west England and one (Mr Courtenay Tracy's) hunting the chalk streams of Hampshire, Wiltshire and Dorset. So popular was the sport that 15 additional packs were formed between 1890 and 1907. The hounds were rough-coated, mostly of Welsh extraction. Summer was the season, and the followers, of course, went dismounted.

The otter was found by its overnight drag, the trail of scent left on the herbage of the meadows and banks of the streams by which it travelled to reach a holt (refuge) after its night's frogging or fishing. After being bolted from the holt, it was hunted along the waterways and the meadows lying between them, usually seeking seclusion on its way in other holts. Hunting all-rounders said that otterhounds possessed the most beautiful cry of all hounds.

63 Sir Henry Bromley and the Kendal. These hounds drew the Derwent and its tributaries, the Esk and other Yorkshire rivers.

OPPOSITE
64 Followers of the Crowhurst over a flooded river bank, near Edenbridge, Kent.

65 Hounds on the line of their quarry in 1898.

66   Gone to ground: The Cheriton hunt by the Yeo, near Barnstaple, Devon.

67   After a kill: The Master of the Cheriton presents a pad to a delighted visitor.

Harehunting

Harehunting, which is probably the oldest branch of venery conducted for pure sport, had a much greater following than many of the other country sports. By Victoria's reign the slow and heavy Old English harrier, descended from the Gascons and Talbots, which the eighteenth-century squires kept, had given place to a miniature (18 to 21 inches at the shoulder) of the active hound (23 to 24 inches) with stamina and drive, as well as nose and cry, which Meynell first bred. In 1903 there were 150 recognised packs of harriers in England and Wales.

The beagle, which was followed on foot, was a still smaller replica of the breed, standing 14 to 16 inches at the shoulder. Beagling, although it, too, had its strict code of conduct, its traditions and shibboleths, was more the poor man's hunting, less the squire's than the townsman's recreation, and more a middle-class than an aristocratic sport.

Owing to changes in the social structure and the growth of the towns, a great revival of beagling took place in the second half of the nineteenth century. The centre of this revival seems to have been the suburban fringes of Surrey, south Middlesex and north-west Kent. Were it not for photographs, such as the ones in these pages, to support the fact, it would be rather difficult to envisage the pony traps and hacks converging for meets at, say, Kingston and Croydon, alongside the train contingents from Victoria and Charing Cross, the male supporters in tight Norfolk jackets and leggings, the women in nicely-tailored tweed coats, voluminous hats, multi-buttoned boots and layers of ankle-length skirts, tripping across the deep plough by Surbiton. Only the hunt staff, in green jackets and stockings, white breeches and black velvet caps, bore much resemblance to the beaglers we know today.

From the 1890s onwards beagle packs were springing up wherever the hare thrived – by 1895 there were 18 – while that other miniature harehound, the long-backed, long-eared basset, made its debut as a hunting hound in 1891, when Major Godfrey Heseltine formed the Walhampton hunt.

The hare owns a weaker scent than the fox or deer, describes a circular, often twisting, course, and shows great cunning in throwing off her pursuers, so hounds are comparatively slow to work out her line. Thus the followers, especially the dismounted beaglers, who could climb wire barriers, probably saw a good deal more of the hound-work than foxhunters and staghunters.

68 Followers of the Peppard Farmers and their wives going to the meet.

HARRIERS

69 Lady Master from Ireland: Miss Isa McClintock of the Tynan and Armagh.

70 Pack with a bloodhound cross: the Sandhurst.

71 The Sandhurst after a kill.

BEAGLES

72 A Sussex hunt. Mr and Mrs Goff with the Wooddale.
These were regarded by the pundits of the early 1900s
as 'the most effective pack of beagles in the world'.

73 University Pack: the Trinity Foot in 1880. Rowland Ward, the Master (seated centre), went on to Cambridge from Eton where he had also been Master and huntsman of the beagles. 'I think he must have made a compact with the dons', said a Cambridge friend, 'as he certainly never wasted many hours in attending lectures, chapel or hall'. Ward was afterwards Master of two Shropshire packs of foxhounds: the Wheatland and North Shropshire.

74 Military Pack: the Colchester Garrison Beagles in 1895. Established in 1861, this hunt followed in the footsteps of Parson Honywood, who bred the ancestors of the modern beagle, hunting the same part of Essex. The Master, Captain Bramwell of the 58th Regiment, is on the right.

75 Family pack of pocket-beagles. The Earl of Hopetoun (afterwards 2nd Marquess of Linlithgow) and his son with their West Lothian miniatures.

76 Followers of the Royal Rock in hot, but impeded, pursuit. Founded in the 1840s in the Wirral of Cheshire, the Royal Rock is the oldest beagle hunt in the world.

77 A Yorkshire pack at the kill: Mr Butcher's near
Sheffield, 1908.

Coursing

Hare coursing – tracking hares with greyhounds, by sight rather than by scent – had been elevated from a farmer's to a gentleman's pursuit towards the end of the eighteenth century, and was soon popular all over Britain. The sport was competitive from the beginning, the standard practice being that, when the beaters put up a hare, she was given a 60 yards start before the greyhounds were slipped from the leash. A mounted judge awarded points on the greyhounds' skill in turning the hare as well as for their speed and adroitness at the kill.

The coursers' Derby, the Waterloo Cup, was instituted in 1836, and the National Coursing Club in 1858. The breeding of the greyhound was no less a serious scientific matter than that of the foxhound, and the *Greyhound Stud Book* was established in 1882.

78 1898: In the slips for the Waterloo Plate.

79 'King' of the coursing scene: the Duke of Leeds (centre) with his trainer, handler and champion greyhound, Lapal.

80 Finalists for the 'Blue Riband of the Leash': Mr E. Rogers's Black Fury and the Duke of Leeds's Lapal about to be slipped for the Waterloo Cup.

Falconry

The hawk, as well as the hound, had been a beast of the chase in England since Saxon times, but the difficulties and expenses of training birds of prey to take game mammals and birds were put in the shade with the development of the sporting gun. Although essentially a specialist subject during the Victorian and Edwardian era, falconry did attract greater interest then among countrymen than it does now. The following photographs show hawks hooded and unhooded; being worked with dogs to fly at either fur or feather; at the lure; and on a weathering stand.

Most men who were attracted to hawking in the reign of, say, Henry VIII or Elizabeth I would probably have become keen game-shots had they been born in the time of William IV or Queen Victoria.

81 The Hon. Gerald Lascelles with hawk and spaniel. Son of the 4th Earl of Harewood and President of the Old Hawking Club for 35 years, Deputy Surveyor of the New Forest and a Fellow of the Zoological Society, he was regarded as 'the greatest expert on hawking in Great Britain'.

82　Hawking with a kestrel: preparing to hood.　　83　Blue Foot hooded, 1898.

84 Casting a falcon at partridge.

85 Goshawking with a dog, 1899. The quarry here were rabbits, pheasants and water-hens.

OPPOSITE
87   A falconry correspondent: Major Hawkins Fisher, who wrote regularly on the subject for *Country Life*.

88 Ready for the field: peregrines prepared for rook hunting.

OPPOSITE
89 Champion goshawk: Mr J.L. Newman with Shâyâ, 1897.

90   On the weathering stand: Mr C. Eustace Radclyffe
and his harks.

Shooting

The sophisticated shot-gun and cartridge we know today were new toys to the Victorians. By 1820 the flint-and-steel igniter had been replaced by the fulminating detonator. In the 1850s came the first breech-loaders, and in the 1870s the first hammerless guns, choke bores and pure steel barrels, along with Mr Eley's 'complete cartridge'. So the art and the methods of game shooting improved, too. The musketeer of the eighteenth century walked up his game individually, shooting over dogs. Then came the first form of *battue*, the walking in line through the coverts and roots, still with comparatively easy shots, close behind the targets. From this, with the speedy reloading allowed by the breech-loader, came the more advanced *battue*, the game in this case being driven towards the guns by beaters, and rendering, in particular, the more sporting shot, the high, head-on bird.

The clearance of woodlands, scrubland and marsh in the interests of agriculture increased the partridge and hare populations, but reduced the pheasant, which was soon seen as the English breech-loader's most desirable quarry. From as early as 1800, the squire, to whom well-stocked coverts were really important, knew a good deal about hand-reared pheasants. By the middle of the century, the practice of putting fresh stocks into the wild from release-pens was widespread, and by the 1880s the science of incubator breeding was mastered.

In landowning circles, in lowland Britain, pheasant (and, to a lesser extent, partridge) shooting soon became the close rival and competitor of foxhunting. For the shoot-owner who had spent large sums of money in putting down birds and creating extra cover for them, perhaps by planting rhododendron, laurel, conifer and other exotics, scarcely welcomed invasions of horses and hounds from his Master of Foxhounds neighbour during the last three months of the year, which was the best of the shooting season. On the other side of the coin, foxes were not plentiful in those days, and foxhunters regarded every game-keeper as an incorrigible vulpicide. (Some still do.) A host of sportsmen were foxhunters and game-shots, too, but many of the really dedicated riders to hounds regarded the *battue*-shot (who took little exercise, thought the foxhunter, but only walked from covert-side to covertside, while the keepers and beaters did the work of the day) as no real countryman. Conversely, the ardent born-and-bred game-shot poured scorn on the parvenu or popinjay foxhunter.

While the hunt meet, like the parish church, was

the rendezvous for all social classes – the standing of each person more or less identified by his dress – the country-house covert shoot provided an exclusive recreational meeting-point for the aristocracy and squirearchy. To lay on a good shoot and to be a good shot, like being 'a good man to hounds', were singular distinctions in the days of Queen Victoria and her son. The Prince of Wales had been a keen foxhunter, but as he grew older his enthusiasm for riding declined, while his passion for shooting waxed, until, when he was on the throne, it became almost his exclusive outdoor winter pastime.

Sandringham, deep in the leading partridge county, Norfolk, was already a good shooting estate when Edward bought it in 1862, and he made it into one of the best three or four pheasant shoots, too. He liked to see a great many pheasants rising high over the guns, with enormous bags to show for it. Also, loving protocol and luxury, he set a new style for patrician shooting parties, in which bored wives came out to join the guns for gargantuan picnic luncheons, in which shooting days led to evenings of somewhat heavy and formal entertainment. From the 1860s onwards he was the leader of fashionable society, so shooting hosts everywhere followed his example. Men like Lords de Grey, Ripon and Walsingham, and Sir Ralph Payne-Gallwey, the best and most prolific shots of their day, regarded shooting as one of life's very few really serious activities.

At the other end of the scale, the relaxation of the Game Laws towards the end of Victoria's time meant that others besides landowners were beginning to enjoy their shooting, too, albeit their quarry was the humbler (though often more sporting) pigeon, hare and rabbit. Those who obtained permits to go wild-fowling, goose and duck shooting on an offshore stretch, at ponds or on the marsh, might see sport of the highest order, as well as enjoying the fascination of the wild and solitary places in which flighting takes place. Moreover, particularly on the Norfolk Broads, there was still punt-gunning, stalking flocks of wild-fowl across the water with the long, large-bored shot-gun.

With the improvement of the sporting gun, the

INSTRUCTIONAL

92   Training spaniels in Scotland.

93   At shooting school. 'Fitting – Elevation', from the same book.

LEFT
91   'Carrying a Gun: safe, dangerous and safe', from *Game and Gunroom Notes* (1900) by 'Blagdon'.

grouse moor, whose denizens were thought to fly fastest of all, soon drew the sassenach sportsman to Yorkshire and the Scottish Highlands in August and September. For with the invention of the breech-loader, it did not much tax the imagination of the Victorian country gentleman to envisage the thrill of driven grouse. The tone set at Balmoral in August was like that at Sandringham from September to January and, just as the railways helped the townsman fox-hunter, so they swiftly steamed the grouse-shot to the north. Moor owners learned to burn their heather, to improve the habitat, and to build butts like tactical palisades.

Birds were shot by the hundreds. While 30 or 40 brace in a day had been considered a good bag for walking up, now, with driving, it was 200 to 300 brace in a day. Moor-owners were also finding that grouse were more profitable than sheep, so crofting declined and shooting rents soared.

94 A large class of setters at school.

95 · Training setters: at the point.

96 The Prince of Wales (afterwards Edward VII) (*seated, centre*) in his prime. An 1860s group.

97 Four decades later: a studio
picture of Edward VII posed for his
favourite sport.

98 The King with his loader at a Norfolk shoot. One of his ambitions was that Sandringham should be the finest shooting estate in Britain. Holkham, its neighbour, was always better.

99 King Edward (right) and his son, the Prince of Wales. A scene between drives at Hall Barn, Beaconsfield, where the host was Lord Burnham.

100 Edward's son in the grouse butts at Balmoral. The Prince of Wales, afterwards King George V, was said to be one of the four best shots in the country.

101 King Alfonso XIII of Spain was a regular guest at English Royal shoots. Shooting 'British' was *de rigeur*: his gun was a Purdey, his clothes Savile Row.

102 A Sandringham Shooting Party in 1899. The Prince of Wales (afterwards Edward VII) stands at the centre right. The Princess of Wales is seated third from the left, with Princess Victoria of Wales on the extreme left, Princess Mary third from the right and the Empress of Germany second from the right. Prince George (afterwards George V) stands fourth from the right and the German Emperor, Kaiser Wilhelm, sixth from the right. Standing behind the Princess of Wales is the Duke of Cambridge.

103 Luncheon during a Dorset shoot.

104 At Mount Juliet, Kilkenny. The Hon. Mrs Hugh McCalmont swings onto her bird.

105 The Marquess of Winchester, with his two loaders, as the Earl of Leicester's guest in a Holkham wood, 1898.

106   The Marquess of Ripon in his pony-cart. He was
widely considered to be the best shot of his generation.

107 Lord Ripon's game wagon at Studley Royal.

109 Changing guns at a pheasant shoot, also at Highclere. A very fine, if very corpulent, shot: Prince F. Dhuleep Singh.

108 The Earl of Carnarvon at his own shoot, at Highclere, Berkshire. His loader is all set to change guns.

110   The same Prince: 'Rabbit forward!'

111   On the grouse moor, January 1898.

112   The Holkham ammunition cart. Its owner, the Earl of Leicester, is the seated figure.

113 All round observation? Waiting in a grouse butt.

114 Grouse-shooting over pointers. The dogs are what is known as 'backing' one another, a method of teamwork said to have been started by the British.

115 More teamwork between gun
and loader. Changing guns on Captain
Radclyffe's Dorset shoot.

116 The loader ducks while the
gun takes a partridge behind.

117 Waiting. Colonel W.E. Brymer, MP for South Dorset.

BELOW
118 Waiting. Mr C. Keigwin at Old Buckingham Hall, Mr Lionel Robinson's shoot, October 1910.

OPPOSITE
119 Waiting. The 'King' of English cricket: W.G. Grace.

OPPOSITE
121 'Partridges over!' At Lord Ashburton's, Alresford, Hampshire.

120 'Over!' Line of guns at a pheasant drive.

122 A Norfolk partridge shoot. The headkeeper briefs the guns.

91

92

OPPOSITE
123 Starting for the hedgerows at Preshaw.

124 A midday break at a small shoot in 1896.

125 Retrieving at Highclere under the eyes of a proud handler, 1901.

ROUGH
SHOOTERS

127 Setting out for a rough shoot? Whether or not this couple 'mean business' they certainly look most unsure of themselves.

128 'Means Business' was the title of this picture in an 1899 issue of *Country Life*.

129 A tradesmen's shoot in the 1860s.

130 Rabbit Shots in 1857: one of the Grundy's *English Views*. Since the Game Act of 1831 rabbits were not counted as game and could be taken by tenants and their servants. But punishment for contravention of the Game Laws remained severe.

131 Rabbit Shots with ferrets, 1901.

132 Rabbit-shooters at Burnham-on-Crouch, Essex, January 1908.

133 Was it wise? A poacher posing for his photograph.

WILDFOWLING

134 An old Norfolk gunman, Fred Barrett, and his two
sons. The Protection of Birds Acts put many of the
commercial wildfowlers out of business towards the end
of the century.

135 Fred comes ashore.

136 Setting out for a day's punt-gunning in East Anglia.

OPPOSITE
137 A punt-gunner taking aim . . .

138 . . . And demonstrating with a sleigh.

139 A wildfowler in his sacking suit – All ready to crouch in a well-camouflaged duck-hole.

Deerstalking

The second of the three Highland field sports reserved for the Scottish grandees and their guests, and for very rich visitors, was deerstalking. 'Deer stalking is a sport which throws all other field sports into the background', William Scrope, author of *The Art of Deer Stalking*, was writing in 1839. 'The beautiful motions of the deer, his picturesque and noble appearance, his sagacity, and the skilful generalship, which alone can ensure success in the pursuit of him, keep the mind in a state of pleasurable excitement . . .'

The rifle progressed far between the turn of the eighteenth century (when it was invented by Samuel Baker) and the end of Queen Victoria's reign. The much advanced Enfield first saw action in the Crimean War, and in the same decade fixed cartridges appeared, with the bullet, charge, priming-powder and detonator combined in a single case. The first breech-loading rifle was followed – in the 1890s – by the bolt

action and magazine, of which the prototype was the Mauser. By this time the deerstalker, who, a century before, was lucky if he could reach the stag's heart at 80 yards, could now do so at 300 yards and more.

The laird, taught as a boy by his father's ghillie, would do his own stalking, spying the hill, and looking for the good wind and safe cover that led him to the final stalk and the careful shot at the unsuspecting stag. Whereas the visitor, only participating in a passive way, would follow the knowledgeable ghillie or professional stalker until, at the end of perhaps a four- or five-hour stalk, placed in a favourable position, he might at last have an opportunity to bring his rifle into action. If he missed, he had at least worked up an appetite.

141   Starting for the hill, in 1901.

OPPOSITE
140   In from the hill, in 1855.

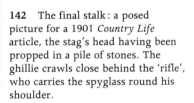

142   The final stalk: a posed picture for a 1901 *Country Life* article, the stag's head having been propped in a pile of stones. The ghillie crawls close behind the 'rifle', who carries the spyglass round his shoulder.

143 Down from the hill in 1901.

144 The end of a woodland stalk: a fine fallow buck. It is hoped that the stalker used solid (not scatter) shot in his 12-bore.

Fishing

The third Scottish pursuit, one which kept the all-round sportsman happy from January to late October, was salmon fishing, the river Tweed being the cradle of this exciting and, at times, hazardous recreation. In the 1860s the English visitor to Scotland was paying as much for his salmon fishing on the Tweed, Dee, Don, Awe, Spey and Tay as he was for his stalking and grouse shooting, although the salmon rivers of England and Wales often produced sport of equally high calibre.

Rod, line, hook and bait had improved considerably since the days of Isaak Walton, and so had the game fisherman's understanding of why salmon and trout took flies and which flies lured them best. When Victoria came to the throne, fly-fishing was all downstream with the wet fly; but, in the 1840s, experiments were being made with a fly that could be floated to resemble an insect. Anglers began to demonstrate the advantages of casting upstream (a practice which had in fact been successfully used in the North Country in the late seventeenth century, but ignored elsewhere), and of false casting to keep the fly dry. The art was gradually made more effective by such innovations as the eyed lip-hook, oil-dressed silk floating line and fine-drawn gut; by the split-cane rod, the spindle reel, and the silk line (replacing horse hair); and by the divided-wing dry fly, a better imitation, which fell lighter on the water. However, the skilful angler was frequently just as successful with worm and other live bait.

The Test was, as it still is, the foremost chalk water. Otherwise the most popular trout rivers were in Derbyshire and Devon. Pisciculture was growing, and riparian owners, often realising that fishing could earn them as much, if not more, than farming, not only stocked their waters heavily, but also removed weed, had their banks mown to the smoothness of lawns and installed seats and shelters, letting out rods at high rents. Game fishing, like stalking and pheasant shooting, was a rich man's diversion. Yet, just as the rabbit and the pigeon served as sport and food for the tenant who enjoyed shooting, so did coarse fish for the man who could not afford salmon and trout. But not even the very rich despised that fighting king of the lakes, the pike, which was normally sought with a spinner dressed either with natural or artificial bait. Sea-fishing with rod and line also became increasingly popular towards the end of the nineteenth century.

That great angler, the diplomat Sir Robert Bruce

145 One of Grundy's *English Views*, 1857. Coarse fishing in windless autumn.

Lockhart, whose happiest fishing days were in the Edwardian era, understood the real attraction of the sport for most fishermen. 'Angling is not slaughter', he wrote in *My Rod, My Comfort*. 'It is not even wholly concerned with the art of catching fish. It is an introduction to one of the most attractive sides of Nature. It not only affords to the city-dweller the beauties of the countryside and the fresh air of the mountain or the meadow; it also instils in him the desire for that contemplation which is now so rare in our robot age. It leads him into the quiet places, where, alone with his thoughts, he may refresh his soul by the side of the running water.' With the quickening pace of industrialisation and technology, the rapidly expanding population and the development of the motor-car, the general sentiment of Bruce Lockhart's words could be applied to all field sports, the solace of which the Victorians and Edwardians probably came to value more and more with the passing years.

146 A fisherman's club setting off in the 1840s. Are the fourth figure from the left and the last on the right reading Isaak Walton's *The Compleat Angler*?

147 'And there was this other huge one – the biggest you've ever seen – that played on the end of me line for two hours, but . . .' (From Grundy's camera again, 1857).

OPPOSITE
148 'I simply don't *believe* it! . . .'

149 Bringing a fish to net in the
Paper Mill pool, Standon,
Hertfordshire, about 1870.

150 The knotty problem of 'which
fly to tie today?'

OPPOSITE
151   A trout on the hook. The River Onny, Shropshire.

152   A salmon played out and ready for the net.

153   Distracted by a cameraman.

154   Pretty; but is she really serious?

155 Pride of an English visitor to Norway: Mrs C.E. Radclyffe with a 53½ lb salmon and grilse.

156 This one was entitled 'My first Jack' in an 1899 *Country Life*, A jack is a small pike.

E

fine haul of pike : Wargrave, Berkshire.

'laying him' : a rainbow trout reared for sport at
resdale Fisheries, 1899.

Safe in a landing net' : at the Wyresdale Fisheries.

More ambitious : with a 20 ft Greenheart salmon rod
Highlands.

Index